AF400453

Between Is and Was

Poems: 1988 – 2008

Karen West

Published by Karen West
Copyright ©2019
All rights reserved

ISBN: 978-0-6484007-4-5

Cover Art by Rachael Lynette French
Book cover design by Anuri Inusha

iii

For BT, who inhabits the spaces between these lines.

Table of Contents

Between Is and Was

Ask a man how he dreams.
Ask him why the colouring in of
the human heart hurts so.
Say you want to go back
for fear of falling.

We are caught, always,
between is and was.
This is part of the human condition;
the hand that grips the heart
will leave marks.

Applied Astronomy

We turn, in moments of gentle
easy pain, to the crazed spinning
of the universe. We'd thought to still
the ever-heaving breast, soothe these little
stabs of distant, hard light
which leave rosy points on a quivering skin,
let the stars bath our wounds in its bright,
purple potion. Still, the sharply-drawn breath,
night weaving adroitly her
bright, perfect garment.

This magic is subtle and exact.
We are, my friend says, pinned
firmly to the underside of the night.

Above, stars throb hotly; night quickens.
In the darkness we each blindly reach
for another's hand, pain stilled
under the eager leaping
of the universe.

Going to Christchurch

In a strange city I lie under
night's damp skin; this is a
different and difficult air.

I know only your absence
This morning I held you,
afraid to let go, inexplicably earthed to
a place and time that never was mine.

Now, in my mind's inscrutable eye,
I see only your image blurred against
the observation deck as we taxied out.

You remain, always, a foreign country;
oh my loved, lost land,
you are obscured beneath a heavy cloud.

Incident in Christchurch

I saw you, coming out of the
corner dairy one evening when I rode
past on a red bus, your head
balanced precariously on that
long, thin neck that is how I
think of you, and your blunt-bobbed
feminist hair flashing and
flying in a liberated wind as you crossed
the crossed roads and my bus went by;
Fiona, playing the intellectual
varsity student to the max—

I didn't wave, call or smile.
You never invited me in.
But anyway, I dreamed of you that
night, sitting on this old bed of mine,
the Port Hills against our dreamful backs.
I'm still waiting for the pink slippers
you never gave me.

The Colour of Happiness

Yes, yes. This is the colour
of happiness; the ship's great
movement into the wind over
the Cook Straight, salt tang
of sea sharply inhaled.
Simply, it is wind and sea,
the direction home,
but this is love's incantation; the
strange, sudden turning of life's
anciently familiar entities to
a great, aching
beautifulness.

Ancestors

Tonight the ancient light
strikes hard; light like stone,
lean.
The stars' cold fires burn close,
and no closer than you
in this warmth of
shared darkness.
The ache of years held
like breath, I stammer my way
between stars and you.
Hid in night's belly,
the ancestors rise.
The planets precess the night.
We seal the dawn with stars.

October Sunday

Under the bright afternoons of
trees, I listen for your leaving,
half-afraid, and willing you to come.

Bees slung slow on zephyrs,
drugged on sun and warm pollen,
thrum and drone about my head.

You do not come.
Your car slips a tall shadow downhill,
away west.

The day is bright, empty hole,
a bleached skin of light taut over
the bones of trees.
A gaunt wind threads leaves.
I go to buy bread.

Love Pome

On the hill, you had crept up, this late
afternoon, dark glasses and all, and

tears I thought; nothing came out right – cloud
and light ill-at-ease, and I, like some

sucked in breath I thought I would
burst. Inside could neither sit nor stand

so cried, dream-eyed and pacing knew
some great wheel had turned; fallen or

crawled to this place, here of no returning,
and afternoon of burning.

Watched the warm earth turning.

Town, Friday Night

In the library it is quiet.
Hands like light wind rustle pages.
Children read quietly to
the big clock's tick. I am keeping
our usual time.

Outside, Friday night bustles.
Outside hours slice into night by halves –
segments of dark.
The clock on the wall is round,
like an orange.
I peel a poem while I wait.

The air is as light and warm as the smile
you will give me as I turn to
watch you enter the big glass doors.

Beyond the bright, big window
night ticks over; inside I wait on.
you are coming.

Variations on a Dreme

I
The stars, like moths, brush
against my sleep, attend my bed,
Scorpio risen from the dead.
And you, sleeping beneath his
tail, living-rooms away. Imagine I'm
with you, with you to stay.

II
At 2 am wake to a berserk moon
quartered, throwing around light,
just her way.
On her back, moon cradles
water; rain to come soon,
any day.

III
Scorpio's packed up his show,
tail and all, and fled; stars
fallen around my bed.
Over the hill you sleep, tossed;
me here, writing 4 am love poems to a
frenzy of light-crazed moths.

Villanelle

The heart is cut and dried.
An absolute condition lasts forever.
Love is a wound on the inside.

I did not choose such pride,
but the mind's emotion's clever;
the heart is cut and dried.

Now it is enough to meet your eyes,
find the kindness we have for each other.
Love is a wound on the inside.

There's only so much can be denied
before farce gives way to fervour;
the heart is cut and dried.

The stars cut deep with light untried.
Night burns with lost endeavour—
love is a wound in the inside.

It seems years since I've cried
with such star-crazed fever.
The heart is cut and dried.
Love is a wound in the inside.

Walking on Water

At Tairua the tide is
running fast, running with the
last light. The currents writhe and
turn, uncoil to the
sprats' mad flicker.
Raise the wooden flag, the ferry
will come at five.

The harbour flows fatly out to sea.
I could step out, walk on water
to the other side.
Think instead of
swifter tides, other shores out of reach.
Dispassionately eye
the distant beach.

Blues for a Red Planet

Under a staccato blanket of
stars, night's touch rough,
I do not sleep for thinking of
you, of how Schiaparelli dreamed,
too.

And the red planet does not sleep;
its small albino eye
blinks mildly. Precession aside,
it sidles from view.
I sleep, dreaming as usual,
of you.

Rain in the Hills I

Rain in the hills and
over the city; assiduous,
falling hard like
a hard kiss.

Awake last night, dreamed
of you; no love ever was
like this.

Horizons blur, sky
parts. The rain quickens;
so, the heart.

Rain in the Hills II

Yesterday I walked in the rain
to see you. Not the ends of the earth
but far enough for you, and
to get wet, watch the rain drift
in tall shafts across the grey page
of the harbour, to lean a cool cheek
against the hills.

Going home I stomped on the road
'til someone gave me a lift.
This morning I made you some bread.

Poem for Three Friends

It is early evening. The light is
brittle, dispassionate. Thin needles of
birdsong prick at the evening's taut
skin. I sit in this this difficult chair
that is not my own, knowing

a friend is leaving, a friend is
dying, a friend stands at a great mountain's foot,
gazing out to sea.

Just now, the small injustices
shriek; an impassioned sky flames with
all my sunset longings.

Sunrise at Kohi Point

These clouds the very shape
of a mad dawn, I have kept watch here
some time now, and hour or more.
Below, the sea drifts like light on
wind, wild with morning.

Fuelled on hill and sea, the
sun is coming flaming, will
rocket up, blind these leaping constellations.
Along the beach below, headlights
burn dawn.

You are down there, somewhere,
somewhere along beach's end.
I imagine you, drifting on
sleep's long tide.

Dream me, love.
Here, I've sent you some
alpha waves.

High Tide, Ohope Beach

Stalking the tide,
you, the harbour, on the other side,
green-lipped mussels sleep
beneath the sea's beat; each
thrust of the wave is
a making of slow love,
wet feet.

The sea's edge lips my skin,
laves the senses.
Striated shells writhe to a
wave's tongue darting.

Over on harbour's edge
you are; you'll keep
that wet kiss,
waiting.

On the Beach

You could be anyone,
down there, mooching the white-lipped
Pacific's edge; a distant speck on the lip of the earth.
The sea's rant provides
an impudent landscape for
your own sullen tide.

You want to be alone.
I'm nuzzled into the sun, further back,
waiting your return.
Your small son bullets the sanded distance
between us.

Sky and sea jaunt; both are
today bluer even than you.
Come on girl, you're
out of your league.
Let's go home.

Lines to Sam Hunt, Nightfisherman

At 2 am the night is
black ocean; above, the clouds
trawl for stars. Like you,
I find my poems are written down
between 2 am and dawn.

A poem births itself, the clouds
berthed at some other wharf,
further on.
An ocean of stars!
Between now and dawn,
clouds gone,
I trawl for words.

Love Poem II

Wherever I look you are there.
If you fill every corner of a room,
where can I look?
Your call so raging I fear
the world would turn
and stare.
Bathed in the light of a thousand
stars, I lay my soul bare.
No escape from you, this
charmed, crazed place.
The only way out is in;
forever I see your face.

Storm

Older now, and wiser
than before, I know
it's for the best. Today, almost
called you up, up over those hills,
down by the sea. I know
you are nowhere I want you
to be.

At beach's end, you'll be,
predictably, whipping up
a storm. It's taken weeks.
You've been gone a longer time.

I never did goodbye too
good. All I can do is wish you
safely inland when
the storm comes.

Meeting

Tonight you sit beside me
like a warm mountain. Eyes closed,
I lean toward you, imperceptibly,
a daisy turning its face to the sun.

Outside, night makes its
nonchalant gestures. Intent, pungent
with all its earthy, familiar
scents of pine and jasmine,
the mown grass sticking to our feet,
it seeks our undoing.
Unspoken words throb in the air
between us.

I had thought to lay these small
and ancient agonies. Instead, can
only watch your tail lights recede,
as ever.

I look upward.
Starlight stings my eyes.

Prayer

You cannot bear, anymore
to hear rain on the
roof, wind in the

irredeemable darkness
of your sensate, sentient
private night.

It is this: skin of the
dark, skin of the heart.
It becomes difficult

to hear the anything but the
heart's hard beating.

Moon Poem

The moon hangs over the city, halved
perfectly, sliced whitely, nightly until

no pale limb is hung out slyly to
be admired. I crawl the highway night,

inspired; stop to write. The moon is a young
girl flirting. The stars are very bright.

Waiting for Stars

The sky folds by silky
layer, that sky blue you
all happiness deepening to
untouchable mauve. On
the horizon, night is
a dark raven, crouching.

Wait long enough and the
small, pure fires of your
ancestors will burn. Then
the night will be pizzicato with stars.

You go outside, look up.
The orchestra of the universe
crashes forth.

Dimanche Bleu

The day is unbearably blue.
Ocean quickens to the acrid
tang of morning, the air
is thin and light as glass.

The sudden sharpness thrills.
I can stand, only, in the acute
blueness of the day, breath caught,
blinking at the morning.

Against the clay flesh of the cliffs,
pohutukawas bleed into a
turquoise sky.

Anorexic Girl

It is like walking on water.
Through the hollow and frail-limbed
frame flows an exquisitely pure light,
light enough to lift her,
float her over the heat waves,
keep her from drowning.

In town, an awkward sun
presses me into the pavement.
Do you think, girl, that if you raised
your arms in beautiful, white
wing-beats, you would rise
from the world like a great,
white bird?

Sleepwalking

When I walk this dark, flat land,
I am a small thing, embalmed
in starlight.

I pluck fretfully at the
rumpled eiderdown of night like
a petulant old woman, feeling
my way in the dark.

The rough gestures of small, nocturnal
beasts beckon me out of my hide,
to snuffle sightlessly against the dark.

And always, night performs its
sympathetic magic; an offering of moonlight
on night's mantic altar, a supplication
to the gods of sleep.

I have become a small, blind
night thing. Sometimes I see only
by the light of stars.

On the Beach with Leigh

When we walked out over
the harbour, an afternoon ago,
weeks back, the pohutukawas
groaned above our heads,
their gnarly arms spread,
twisted shadow on cool sand.

Your blue-bottled, diamond-studded
smile was a bright shard
of sunlight. Our faces turned
to the ocean, the light trembled curiously
over a driftwood beach.

Enough
(For Gregg)

You wear your
discontent restlessly,
like an old hair shirt, the familiar skin of a
wrought day settled over
the flesh and battered bone of living.

I want only to say that
when it comes, it comes like
sudden rain, that great, odd moment
of pleasure when, say, the
leaves lift on tiptoe
and dance like angels
across the afternoon—

You have to seize this moment,
freeze it in time.
It becomes enough.

Dairyflat Raindirge

All evening the rain has fallen.
In the dark coming home it
uncurls itself over the night
like a wet dream.

You are further from me than
the dawn. You glow ghostly in
my head, moon behind cloud.

There remains nothing more
for me to do but to
turn out the light, climb
into the this wet, labyrinth night,
be gentled into gathering sleep like
rain moving across the world.

On the Pier

Wide-eyed and dreaming,
we watched the mullet twist in
the tide, in the evening's
last light.

My friend and I drinking an
icy white, the dregs of the sun's light
fingering the stems of our glasses.

And at our feet, the harbour
lapping greenly at the pier, and me,
learning, with the help of a friend,
how to breathe again.

Quark Dreams

The universe has come crawling
in from the night.
It wakes me. It slips in
through the venetian blinds,
furtive, crouching under my bed,
blinking in the dark.

Quarks and electrons dance
in my string theory dreams.
Fields of physics are only
what they seem.
More so in the dark.

I exist in a half world.
Not here, not there.
The moon observes me from the window.
The wave function collapses.
I drift into the perfect symmetry of sleep.
Schrodinger's cat purrs at my feet.

The Three Stages of Grief

You still have power.
You inhabit my dreams like a ghost,
night after night,
unbidden, but not as unwanted
as you can be
and I do not know why
this should be, why
I should now fall again and again
into loving you, even though
at first I was angry
then grieved, a great heaving loss lying
heavy on my sleep.

But pain and happiness are lovers
like we are, at some level,
still. All this time,
you have been my only muse.

So every time I look into the night,
there you still are, somewhere out there,
under Scorpio's tail,
forever precessing my dreams.

Other poetry collections by Karen West

Small Journeys

36

About the Author

Karen West is a native-born New Zealander now living in in Australia. This, her first collection of poems written while she lived in New Zealand, has a strong focus on the images and sensations of the unique New Zealand scenery and experience, and covers themes such as love and loss, small town life and astronomy in the southern hemisphere.

Contact Ms West at quantumgirl65@gmail.com

Printed by Libri Plureos GmbH in Hamburg,
Germany